To Kiki
May each day
peace + love
be with you.

As We Begin Again

Doris Washington

As We Begin Again

POEMS OF INNER PEACE, HEALING, HOPE, AND LOVE

by
Doris Washington

Book Cover & Interior Photographs by Joni Meyers
Author Photograph Supplied by the Author

Copyright © 2022 by Doris Washington.

Library of Congress Control Number: 2022900950
ISBN: Hardcover 978-1-6698-0736-0
Softcover 978-1-6698-0735-3
eBook 978-1-6698-0734-6

All rights reserved. No part of this book may be reproduced or transmitted in any form or by any means, electronic or mechanical, including photocopying, recording, or by any information storage and retrieval system, without permission in writing from the copyright owner.

Any people depicted in stock imagery provided by Getty Images are models, and such images are being used for illustrative purposes only.
Certain stock imagery © Getty Images.

Print information available on the last page.

Rev. date: 02/15/2022

To order additional copies of this book, contact:
Xlibris
844-714-8691
www.Xlibris.com
Orders@Xlibris.com
839094

Contents

Dedication ix
Acknowledgements xi
Foreword xiii

POEMS FOR AUTISM AWARENESS

The Child That Plays Alone 1
My Inspiration 2

AS WE BEGIN AGAIN

As We Begin Again 5
Take Me To Your Place 6
Inner Peace 7
Letting Go 8
Embracing New Life 9
A New Day 10
Beyond The Clouds 11
Direction 12
Happiness 13

FORGIVENESS & HEALING

Healing 19
I Can Always Begin Again 20
The Morning Sun 21
The Wilderness 22
Forgiveness 24
Gathering Stones 25
Alone 26
Accepting 27
Time Heals, And So Does Love 29
You 30

ENDURANCE

Endurance 35
God's Enduring Love 36
Seek Him! 37
The Armor Of God 38
The Most Beautiful Gift 39
In Due Season 40
A Message About Endurance 41

THE SUN SHINES THROUGH

The Sun Shines Through 47
The Storms 48
A Rainbow Of Hope 49
Morning 50
A Ray Of Hope 51
Sunrise 52
Over The Horizon 53
As A Flower Blooms – Hope Lives 54
A Message About Hope 55

PEACEFULNESS

Peace Within 61
May Peace Be With You 62
Whirlwind 63
Peace 64
So Beautiful The River Each Time It Flows 65
The Beauty Of Life 66
God's Peace 67
The Joy In The Morning 68
A Daily Prayer Poem 69

HE IS MY STRENGTH – MY SONG

He Is My Strength - My Song 75
This Day Today 76
I Abide In You 77
The Lord Watches Over Me 78
I Have A Song In My Heart 79
Joy 80
His Everlasting Love 81
A New Day Begins 82
As The Morning Comes 83

ALONG THE WAY

Along The Way 89
Don't Forget To Count Your Blessings! 90
A Friend Is A Treasure 91
A Thanksgiving Message 92
The Angel Inside Of Us 93
Avenues 94
Together 95

ENCOURAGEMENT

A Message About Encouragement 101
I Cannot Stay Where I Am 102
Road Blocks 103
Possibilities 104
The Leap of Faith 105
Words Of Encouragement 106
A Journey Of A Thousand Steps 107
The Beauty Of You 108
A Message About Faith 109

AS WE DISCOVER LOVE

As We Discover Love 115
Beyond The Sunset 116
For The Light Of The World- A Child Is Born 117
A Message About Christmas 118
Our Saving Grace 119
Each Day I Awake 120
A Message About Love 121
The Beauty Of Love 122
Always Love 123
Inspiration 124
Caring 125

Dedication

I dedicate this book to my husband John and son John for their love and support always.

Acknowledgements

I would like to thank my husband John and son John for always their continued love and support, which have made my dreams for the creation of this work possible. I also would like to thank Joni Meyers and many wonderful friends and family who continues to believe in my writings and poetry.

Foreword

As We Begin Again, is a collection of poems that encourages us to discover what we all long for – inner peace. Also, in this collection are poems about finding healing through forgiveness, poems that encourage us to hold on to hope and press forward with faith that better days are just moments away. These combination of poems are inspiring and uplifting to the soul, giving us a positive side to living life, encouraging us to embrace love more in our lives.

In the poem, *As We Begin Again*, I invite you to find inner peace. In the poem, *Forgiveness*, I encourage you to discover that healing begins with forgiveness.

In the poem, *Endurance,* I express that through life's challenges, as we keep the faith and hold on to hope, that life is forever changing, that better days will come. In the poem, *The Child That Plays Alone*, I share my personal experience about my son who has autism, inviting you to his world for a better understanding and awareness. In the poem, *Along The Way,* I share that *Life i*s a journey, which there're many roads you can take, and sometimes there are those friends that we meet not always by chance, but through a divine connection.

And in the poem, *A Message About Love,* I express that as you open your heart to see always with love, inner peace you'll always find.

My hope is that this collection of poems will bless, inspire, and encourage others to live a more positive life.

Poems For Autism Awareness

The Child That Plays Alone
In Dedication to Autism Awareness

He talks to himself, and no one hears what he says.
His activity seems strange and unusual to some.

If only they would see his gift, he could accomplish
More than you know.
If only someone would take the time to explore
What he has.

He could be a great musician, a great artist, a great dancer-
A great athlete.
He has many toys and he plays by himself.
The other children do not understand him.
They do not play with him.

He likes to do the same things other children do.
And yet he is shut out from the world.
He is different, but aren't we all different.

If only someone would play with him.
If only someone would see His Gift!
The Child That Plays Alone

My Inspiration
In Dedication to Autism Awareness

Your smile- I wait for each day.
You are the joy that keeps me going.
And on every wake of each morning-
I'm thankful to God for you.

You teach me so much.
To love the beauty of you.
To love you as you are.
And most importantly
All that you give to me.

I love your uniqueness.
And whether if the day seems cloudy or not-
You bring the sunshine.
You are my inspiration.
I wait each day for – *your smile*.

As We Begin Again

As We Begin Again

The past we cannot forget –
Nor can we relive yesterday.
Only can we learn from mistakes made.
And remind ourselves where we have been.

As we move forward with a new vision
To live life better.
We can start over-
We can start today –
Living more positive –
Not having no regrets –
To appreciate life more.

And to see the blessings at every corner
We turn.
Each day has it challenges.
And it also has its many blessings
For us to be thankful for.
Always inspiring us to live life
More fulfilled –
As We Begin Again.

Take Me To Your Place

Touch me My Father!
Shower me with Your
Goodness and Grace.
Help me stay still in times of trouble,
And for whatever trials I may face.
Take me to Your Place.

Strengthen me in the spirit,
So Your Voice is the only voice I hear.
Stay with me, and talk to me,
Whether it be far or near.
Take me to Your Place.

Anoint me!
Lift me up in Your Spirit.
Help me accept and love others for
Who they are.
Grant me everlasting peace.
And if I stray Lord too far! -
Take me to Your Place!

Inner Peace

There's a place that I long for to be –
That place - inner peace.

Each day as I breathe life –
I seek to live a better way-
To always see the positive
In every situation.

Each day as I breathe life –
I go with the understanding
That the only thing I can change -
Is myself.

Each day as I breathe life –
I find that when I pray -
And always see with love-
Peace fills my heart with joy.

There's a place that I long for to be-
And each day as I breathe life –
I come to understand
That with faith and my trust in God –
That place – *inner peace* – I will always find.

Letting Go

Cleansing in one's soul.
Peace,
And serenity flows.
Hurt,
And pain released.
Your heart at peace.
Love steps in,
As you surrender it to Him.
Letting Go!

Embracing New Life

As you let go of things you cannot change -
You can then turn the page to a better way of living.
As you choose to find fulfillment – inner peace
You'll come to know more and more.

Life is all about the choices you make.
For the only thing you can change is yourself.
When you let go of what is negative –
You also choose to go with love.

And as you embrace new life –
As you give of your heart -
You'll find the spirit of love
Will always follow you -
Encouraging others to love too!

A New Day

I awake from a long sleep,
Yes, a long sleep from loneliness,
Self pity,
And regret.
I no longer choose to taste the bitter tongue
Of the trials of life.

I no longer allow worry, self-doubt,
And negative energy to be the focus of existence.
I no longer starve for others approval,
Opinions and love.

Forgiveness is what I practice.
Patience has become my daily routine.
Love keeps me alive.
And I seek Him always.
As I Start-
A New Day

Beyond The Clouds

As the day awakes-
I move forward to discover
There's always a *blessing*
To encourage me to look-
Beyond the clouds.

Peace within my soul-
I seek more than ever now-
In a vast and ever changing world-
Where negativity abounds.

I feel my heart with love.
And with a positive way of living-
I can see the blessings He gives to me
In every moment of the day.
And I see that life is more beautiful-
More fulfilled this way.
As I look –
Beyond The Clouds.

Direction

Yesterday I cannot change,
But today I can.
And as I awake on this new morning -
I start again.

Mistakes are sometimes made
More often than not.
And I choose not to dwell on what is past.
But right now, I have a choice to live a better way.

Inner peace I so invite to have at all times.
I lean on Him always for guidance- for strength -
Each and every day.

Yesterday I cannot change,
But today I can.
And this choice to live a most positive life -
Is a *direction* I seek more and more.

Happiness

One must be content in what gives them fulfillment –
Happiness.
To make your own choices in life is what's most important -
To finding peace in the decisions that you make.

As you follow your passion in all you wish to be -
Rise above the disappointments –
And never give up.
Peace and joy you'll have.

For when you follow your passion -
Believe with faith –
And answer to your heart –
Happiness – will always be yours.

*As We Recover – As We Gather Stones-
Our Healing Begins. And As We Find Those Things
That Brought Us Joy – We Will Have Again!*

Forgiveness & Healing

Healing

I have endured many storms
That have come and gone.
I let go of the hurt and pain from before.
Although, it has been heavy upon me -
I prayed for strength.
And now as I go on with *hope* -
Each day, I allow time
To begin again.
Thank You Lord! –
I'm Healing!

I Can Always Begin Again

My healing begins through forgiveness.
My hurt- my pain is washed away.
And as I find the *lov*e
Always inside of me -
I can begin again.
I can start anew.

He may close a door-
For another door to open.
And Life's twist and turns
May be too much to bear at times.
But as I lean on Him-
Trust in Him to know
He'll work it all out in time-
Oh! Such peace I find.

And with that I can see a new day
Always starts with me.
To understand what I cannot change
I must surrender it all to – Him.

My healing begins through forgiveness.
My hurt- my pain is washed away.
And as I fill my heart with His Love -
I Can Always Begin Again.

The Morning Sun

Revelations came to me
At the break of dawn.
Realizing many things.
Looking over my life,
How it has been,
Where I am now,
And where I am going.
Letting go of issues from others,
Issues I have, I'm facing
What I can't change.
And I'm moving forward to a new change.
My healing begins.
And I can see clear,
As I see -
The Morning Sun

The Wilderness

Darkness surrounded me -
I could not see the light.
The light was there, but I could not see it.
Assumptions of what I perceived,
Became my reality.
Negative energy kept coming in when I least expected.

Loneliness, bitterness, and despair engulfed my spirit.
I could not breathe.
Then a voice said: "Come with Me."
He talked to me there.
He guided me to a place of peacefulness
That I've never known.
There were many trees to guide me along the way.

They were marked with directions to
Where I was meant to be.
I then began to see the light through the darkness.
The blessings that were always there –
I began to see and receive.

His Love filled me!
His Love engulfed me!
Positive thoughts became my reality.
I was no longer misguided.

The place I was meant to be was not far.
With Him I was not alone.
For with His Light –
He saw me through –
The Wilderness.

Forgiveness

Forgiveness is all about healing
And letting go of the hurt and pain –
Past and present.

Sometimes, one can find it difficult to forgive –
For however deep the wound may be.
Yet, with forgiveness you can find peace –
And invite love to heal your heart.

For as you forgive - you can open your heart
To embrace – *Love!*

Gathering Stones

Recovering from it all,
I pick up the broken pieces
Along the way.
Drifting away far too long,
I now re-group, to get some balance.
And I'm ready to begin again.

There's so much out here
To discover.
And yet I feel uncertain where
I'm going.
Taking it one step at a time,
I seek the desires of my heart.
And my dreams are not far away
To be fulfilled.

Recovering from it all,
I pick up the scattered pieces
Along the way.
Drifting away- far too long,
I now re-group, to get some balance.
And I'm ready to begin again.
Out Here-
Gathering Stones

Alone

Alone does not always stand for lonely.
Sometimes it's a great healing- that space
To grow.

Alone sometimes helps you with a great
Sense of focus and perspective.
And the trials can be triumphs.

Alone sometimes helps you stay encouraged,
Empowering you to many heights- many possibilities.

Alone is a period each of us experiences for however
Long it may be.
Overcoming barriers -moving forward with belief
In one's self.

Alone does not always stand for lonely,
For it can take you to other places, expanding
Your horizons,
And finding you're not-
Alone.

Accepting

Healing from the hurt and pain.
I cry no tears like rain.
I Am- Accepting

Letting go of things that don't change.
Cleaning out the junk in my heart-
Only to rearrange.
I Am- Accepting

To Rearrange! To Rearrange!
Putting things in priority.
Seeing Blessings, and no excess baggage I carry.
I Am- Accepting

Moving away from disappointments.
Picking up the broken pieces to begin again.
Never giving up on life.
Loving who I am.
Believing I am my best friend.
I Am- Accepting

Not wearing a frown.
Carrying only a smile.
Giving my worries to God.
And all the while.
I Am-
Accepting!

Time Heals, And So Does Love

Time heals wounds,
And so does *Love*.
Time gives us a better perspective,
A chance to see things differently.
For that can only be *Love*.

Always forgiveness releases
The hurt, the pain before.
For one's life doesn't always stay the same.
Things can change in minutes, hours, and years.
The good news is there's always a chance
To change things each day of your life.

Yes, time heals wounds.
But it's always the choices we make.
For as we invite the love to come within,
As we start to see the goodness in everyone.
We'll find that time not only heals-
And So Does Love.

You

Silence after the storm,
The storm that was raging
So long.
The *Storm* is over now.
Time to start a new direction.
Time to find a new sense of purpose.
Leaving what is familiar,
Even with new ventures to seek.
The old will not be again.
And taking it one step at a time,
It will be alright.
For I'm here,
Alive, like I have never been before.
Thank you, Lord!
I begin here! -
I begin with-
You!

*Through Forgiveness The Light Shines Through.
And As Our Healing Begins – Love We So Embrace!*

Endurance

Endurance

There're always obstacles through life's journey.
And its how one faces the challenges to continue on.
Even at those times when all seems hopeless -
And you find it difficult to endure.

Never Give Up!
Pray!
And find strength to keep pressing on.
For with each new day there're endless possibilities –
That may come at any time.

It's always about having faith to endure all things –
And to trust in God to see you through to carry on.
Faith is –
Enduring!

God's Enduring Love

There'll be days full of clouds in the skies.
And there'll be days the sun shines so beautiful.
And for every moment we have- each day-
We can be thankful.

Life has its challenges-
Its *Joys*.
His Miracles are all around us
In the wake of each new day.

And as we endure and find strength for the day.
As we hold on to *faith* -
There's always *Hop*e to see us through every storm.
There's Always-
God's Enduring Love.

Seek Him!

I put my trust in God!
For with all the storms raging
All around me – I seek Him more
Than ever before.

For it doesn't matter how many storms keep coming.
It doesn't matter if there's no relief in sight –
I Pray!
Even with yesterday's past that brought so much rain -
Today, the sun shines so beautiful.

He works through all things large and small.
His Promise is that His Mercy and Love is Everlasting!
He Is Able!

I put my trust in God!
For with all the storms raging all around me-
More and more –
I Seek Him!

The Armor Of God

Only by faith I go forward.
For all things are possible with God.
And through the storms
He's always there.

He gives me favor to know-
That no weapon formed against me
Shall prevail.
No weapon formed against me
Will take my – *Joy*.
No weapon formed against me
Will devour my – *Faith*.
No weapon formed against me
Will destroy my – *Hope*.
No weapon formed against me
Will not keep me from *Praising Him!*

Yes! All things are possible
With God!
For He gives me Favor! -
And with the blessings He so brings-
Through every trial – through every- *Joy!*
Only by *Faith* I go forward.

The Most Beautiful Gift

Life itself is a blessing.
And there'll be disappointments
Along the way.

And for every –
Challenge you so endure -
Find the joy and peace within.

Hold on to every blessing -
And begin to love you.
Follow your passion -
No matter where it takes you.

For each day you have begins
With you and how you live life.
And the most beautiful gift
Is the *Love* you give each
And every time you breathe – *Life!*

In Due Season

When I think about all the blessings
He brings.
When I think about His Grace- His Love,
I can only stay where He wants me to be.
I cannot doubt Him,
No matter what,
No matter the challenges.
And when the storms come,
And it seems as though they will not pass,
I look up to Him to know
He's my help -
He's my friend.
And whatever my desires,
I know He will grant.
Yes,
Always-
In Due Season

A Message About Endurance

Sometimes, storms will come when you least expect.
And as you hold on to hope –
Believe with faith-
You will endure.

With life's many challenges -
And as storms come and go -
Pray for God's Strength –
His Mercy –
His Love.
For better days are just moments away.

With Hope – We Can Rise Above Any Storm –
For Before We Know – We Have Already Reached The Shore!

The Sun Shines Through

The Sun Shines Through

For when the clouds are heavy upon us-
The sun shines through.
Through the joys –
And through the most difficult of times -
The sun shines through.

Let's hold on to hope to see us through
Life's most greatest challenges.
And may we believe with faith -
That whatever problems arise -
We will get through it.
For as time shows us so well -
Always-
The Sun Shines Through.

The Storms

He didn't promise they'll always be days of sunshine.
For rainy days do come.
And sometimes they may seem to last forever.

Believe He will always be there
To get you through any storm.
Yes! – any storm imaginable.

Sometimes storms may be a test of one's faith.
For as you trust in Him-
To know with no doubt-
All will be alright- no matter how heavy the storm.

He will carry you when you cannot carry yourself.
He will bring you through.
Even if it seems hopeless.
Know that He is *hope* to hold on to.

He didn't promise they'll always be days of sunshine.
But He did promise
He will always be there through it all.
For He will bring a *Blessing* through –
The Storms.

A Rainbow Of Hope

Storms do come your way.
Some seems as though they last forever.
But hold on to hope through the storms-
As they come through.

Hold on to His Everlasting Mercy – His Love.
And always Pray!
Know that each day you have – is a blessing –
And resolve through it all.

Always stay in faith and believe-
That what seems hopeless -
He is the Hope for you to never doubt
His Amazing Love.

Storms do not last forever.
And His Love will see you through every storm.
Hold on to the Blessing -
A Rainbow of Hope –
He brings each day you breathe – *Life!*

Morning

Yesterday has come and gone.
Tomorrow brings promise,
And always hope.
And for now,
I'm doing alright.
Yes! - I'm doing just fine.
And each breath I take,
It's Good.
Yes! - It's All Good!
Hello-
Morning!

A Ray Of Hope

For no matter how hopeless things
May come to be- there's hope
To always believe that better times
Will and shall come.

Take each day as it comes.
Believe each day can bring
The light through the darkness.

Hope is never giving up no matter
What comes your way.
Each day you have is a blessing.
For blessings comes through
Joyous moments and through
The most challenging of life's experiences.

As you hold on to that ray of hope -
To believe that better times will
And shall come, you'll find
The blessings along the way.

For in those darkest of days –
And the storms are heavy upon you -
Believe there's always *hope* to hold on to -
Always!

Sunrise

As the sun rises each morning so new.
I Thank God for another day.
For on this day I choose to live each moment
Even better than the day before.
And right now- I have a chance to do all that
I hope for- dream for.

Life is so precious.
Each moment counts.
And what's more beautiful for each day I awake -
I can change things always for the better.
Whether it's to make things right with someone.
Or whether it's to fulfill my true passion in life -
Each time the sun rises-
Each Morning So New.

Over The Horizon

Even if the rain seems to last forever-
The sun will always shine through.
Always there's a test in your faith.
And time shows that so well.

There are no barriers you cannot overcome.
And as each morning the sun rises -
Each night the sun sets -
Stay Encouraged!

Hold on to your faith.
Find strength through the day.
Believe all things work out.
Press forward with Hope.

For the rain may seem to last forever-
But as you look-
Over the Horizon-
The sun always shines through.

As A Flower Blooms – Hope Lives

There's always Hope to hold on to.
And each time the rain comes-
The sun will shine even more brighter.

Sometimes life may throw us a curve.
All of a sudden it may seem difficult
To grasp.
But with hope and always faith-
We can know joy in every precious moment.

For as we have each morning-
As we awake each day –
Each time the sun rises –
Each time a flower blooms-
There's always hope to hold on to.
For-
As A Flower Blooms – Hope Lives.

A Message About Hope

For whatever storms that comes your way-
Remain hopeful.
Through every storm -
The sun always shines through.

With hope – you'll find strength to see it through.
Trust in God.
He brings the light through the darkness.
He will never leave you alone.

For each morning you awake-
For every day you have -
And whatever storms that comes your way –
Always remain hopeful – that better days will come.

*With Each New Day – Believe With Hope –
The Sun Will Always Shine Through!*

Peacefulness

Peace Within

Through the wake of the morning-
Through the many hours of the day –
And as the night begins to fall –
Peace within my soul I seek for.

As every storm that comes my way-
Through the disappointments –
And the greatest of challenges that
Always test my faith –
Peace within my soul I seek for –

And Yes! -
More than ever before –
Peace within my soul I find –
Always when –
I Pray!

May Peace Be With You

As the morning breaks on this most beautiful day-
I rest my heart with no heavy sorrow.
Only such wonderful thoughts I hold dear of you.
And with every joyous moment while you were here -
I hold on to the understanding it was your time to go.

Each day I find peace.
I cherish the times no matter how brief.
I am blessed with the joy you brought –
And much more.

Sometimes we may not understand why
Those we love cannot stay.
But as we cherish what they have given
To us- whether it be inspiration or – Joy! –
We can find peace.

And as each day passes –
As we remember the beauty of what
They brought to our lives -
As we remember them -
May Peace Be with You.

Whirlwind

In a whirlwind spinning
Out of control.
Finally stepping back
To see what direction
You're taking.
Is it good?
Is it right?
Understanding what is meant to be.
Revaluating all of it since it started,
And where it is now.
Then to realize for self,
That Acceptance is Peace.

Peace

Sometimes forgiving can be difficult,
Especially when feeling hurt and disappointed.
Sometimes even when the world is unkind,
Being right doesn't hold too much.
Letting go can be such a wonderful feeling,
And the world will seem much nicer.
It's a matter of perspective.
It's a matter how to deal with it
In your mind- in your heart- in your soul.
To let go with no hesitation for the simple
Reason to be at -
Peace.

So Beautiful The River Each Time It Flows

The river is so beautiful each time it flows.
And on this day, I seek You more.
There's a peace that I so find -
As the waters of the river flows so calm - so serene.

All is well.
And when the challenges come,
I seek You more than ever in this quiet place
Where the river flows.
I hold on to hope that tomorrow will be better.
For today is a test of my faith.

Things do not stay the same.
Each day is new.
And there's always a blessing You bring
Each day in one's life.

On this day I seek You more.
I Hold On.
I Hold On To- You!

Oh! How beautiful the river-
Each Time It Flows.

The Beauty Of Life

Sometimes there are moments
Through life's journey things just happen
With no explanation.
And I have found that when I truly let go –
To come to peace –
Life is so beautiful.

For when things are not going so well-
And when it seems as if all is falling apart-
I find only when I let go of those things
I cannot change- I come to peace.

At this moment, I come to peace.
For no matter, what I go through.
No matter the joys and the trials-
I come to peace.
And more than ever I find-
Life is So Beautiful.

God's Peace

When the world seems too much to bear,
Too much to grasp,
I seek Your Peace within.
I find Your Strength to sustain me at all times.
And I pray more than ever before.
For it's Your Peace that flows like
The water along any brook or stream.
It's Your Peace that makes the new fallen snow
So beautiful on a brisk winter's morning.
It's Your Peace when the birds sing so lovely
On a warm summer's day.
It's Your Peace when the leaves fall
So gently in October.
It's Your Peace so beautiful.
When the world seems too much to bear,
Too much to grasp -
I look up to know You're always there.
With You-
Such Peace-
I Find.

The Joy In The Morning

Life has its storms.
And there's always the joy in the morning
That can carry you through the night,
And the next day after that.
When problems arise,
And there seems no relief,
Hold on to the joy.
Let the sun shine through.
Believe it all takes care of itself,
No matter the storm.
And you'll find peace.
For Life has its Storms.
And there's always –
The Joy In The Morning!

A Daily Prayer Poem

Dear Lord, I Pray -
You give me strength for each day.
Guide me when I'm lost.
Hold my hand when I'm afraid.
Heal me from the hurt and the pain.
Help me let go of things I cannot change.
Anoint my spirit to always do what is right.
Teach me- Show me - Your Way.
Dear Lord-
This I Pray!

*Inner Peace I Invite To Have At All Times.
Yesterday I Cannot Change – But Today I Can.
For To Live A Positive Life –
Is A Direction I Seek More and More.*

He Is My Strength – My Song

He Is My Strength - My Song

Through the wake of the new day-
And through the calm of the evening
I seek Him –
I lean on Him.
He's my strength - my song.

I sing Praises to Him.
I'm thankful for His Blessings -
And I trust in Him through
The storms He carries me through.

He's never forsaking.
All He ask is that you put your trust in Him.
The Lord! -
He's, *my strength* –
He's, *my song!*

This Day Today

This day today,
I took a moment to breathe,
To laugh,
And to smile.

This day today,
I saw hope through the disappointments,
To stay always encouraged.

This day today,
I focused on the goodness,
To know all gets better if one believes.

This day today,
I practiced the act of Faith,
To keep going,
To never give up.

This Day Today,
I took a moment to breathe,
To laugh,
To smile,
And to Pray!
This Day Today!

I Abide In You

You are the *joy* in the morning.
You are the *strength* I need each day.
You are the *wind* that holds me through every storm.

You are the *light* through the darkness.
You are the *sunshine* through the rain.
You are the *anchor* when the waters overflow.
And when *danger* is near,
Your arms surround me to know
You will never leave me.

For it's my *faith* that keeps me going.
It's my *trust* in You.
The reassurance,
The peace within my soul
That wherever I am-
Dear Lord! -
I believe things that seems impossible
Are possible always-
With You!

The Lord Watches Over Me

I do not fear the darkness at night.
For the sparrow stays within my sight.
Oh! How The Lord Watches Over Me.

I do not fear the arrows that come at me
During the day.
For the Lord is all around,
He is with me in every way.
The Lord Watches Over Me.

I do not dwell too long in despair.
For I know I am in The Lord's Care.
The Lord He Watches Over Me.

I trust in the Lord - I hold on to His
Unchanging Hand.
For when I am weak, He helps me stand.
The Lord Watches Over Me.

I will stay in the House of The Lord,
He will never leave me.
For I know with Faith,
He is with me through eternity.
Oh! How The Lord Watches Over Me.

I Have A Song In My Heart

I hear the birds Sing.
I receive the Lord's Blessing.
Oh! How beautiful the Sound.
God's Presence is all around.

I sing no sad song.
Unhappiness does not last long.
With such joyful tears,
I've learned through the years.

Life is precious and worth living.
The best of me I keep giving.
I trust in God always.
Peace,
Joy,
And Love I carry with me
The rest of my days.
For-
I Have a Song in My Heart!

Joy

For every moment of the day,
And no matter what I go through -
I find – *Joy*!

For it's the *Joy* that makes my heart Sing!
It's the *Joy* that encourages me
To keep going.

It's the *Joy* that inspires me with hope,
Even when I feel discouraged about today,
I stay encouraged for a better tomorrow.

It's the *Joy* that gives me strength
To endure the challenges –
The disappointments along the way.

It's the *Joy* that lifts me up in spirit-
To believe within my heart – and my soul-
That nothing is impossible.

It's the *Joy* - I hold on to –
No matter what I go through-
With every moment of any given day!

His Everlasting Love

There's always *a blessing* He brings,
In every moment of each day.
For no matter what life brings
From day to day,
And whether it seems hopeless
Beyond despair,
Know that His Love will never fail us,
And that we can find strength for the day.

As we hold on to *Hope* -
As we believe tomorrow will be better –
May we trust in *Faith-*
That His Mercy-
His Everlasting Love will be there-
Always –
For every moment of each day.

A New Day Begins

Life is always changing-
And a new day begins.
Life has its challenges,
Its joys.
The good news is while
You're here there's always
The opportunity to live
Each day as if it's your last.
Take each experience
And always see the blessing
Behind everyone.
Sometimes things don't always
Work out as we hope.
But never give up on *Hope*.
Sometimes the rain comes
To make room for the sun to shine
Even brighter.
For life is always changing-
And-
A New Day Begins!

As The Morning Comes

At this moment I start anew-
Releasing all worries-
I find strength for the day.
For with You –
I can overcome any obstacle.

And as I face each day-
I Pray-
Leaving all with You!
I see the joy more than before.
And for each day You give me-
I thank You more each time –
The Morning Comes.

*He's My Joy In The Morning –
He Carries Me Through Every Storm.
For He's The Reassurance That He's Always There.
He's My Strength – My Song!*

Along The Way

Along The Way

There're those friends you meet through
Your travels.
Those special people who are there
To guide you through life's journey.

And whether you see them again,
Remember that sometimes people
Cross our paths for a reason.

Sometimes, you meet those friends
Who gives you support and encouragement
When you need it the most.

Sometimes, you meet those special people
To help you through a period of your life
That was most difficult.

Sometimes, people come into your life
To be a blessing –
A divine connection.
Those Special People – Those Friends -
Along the Way.

Don't Forget To Count Your Blessings!

When at times things are not going right.
Just remember to hold on to the good things
In your life.
Don't Forget To Count Your Blessings!

When there are those you find
Do not think of you.
Remember the ones who do.
Don't Forget To Count Your Blessings!

When you find the world is not kind.
Look for the *rainbow* in the sky-
And know you will be fine.
Don't Forget To Count Your Blessings!

And when you cannot find
What you are looking for-
Look around.
And be thankful the Lord has for you-
Greater things in store.
Don't Forget to Count Your Blessings!

A Friend Is A Treasure

A friend never stops caring –
Even when you give up on self –
A friend never gives up on you.

A friend always supports –
Sees you through the worst of times –
And celebrates with you in the best of times.

A friend doesn't always agree with you on all things.
Yet, with kindness and love a friend always
Speaks the truth.

A friend never stops caring –
Always there through it all.
A friend is a – *treasure!*

A Thanksgiving Message

It's a November's Blessing!
Being thankful for the gathering
Together of family and friends.
It's a celebration of love and the joy of giving.

It's a remembrance and embracing traditions past-
Cherishing precious moments –
Counting our blessings -
And always thankful for the blessings
He Brings -
Each Time –
Each Year-
Thanksgiving!

The Angel Inside Of Us

Finding that angel inside of us –
With the simple act of kindness can do
So much for the soul.
For with a smile, you give someone can make
For a much brighter day.

Helping a neighbor in time of need that
Was unexpected, can make a difference
In one's life.
And sometimes just being a friend to someone -
Can change one's perspective how to see and live life.

As we find the angel inside of us –
We give the best of ourselves-
We answer to our hearts –
We make the world a better place.

For as more of us give that simple act of kindness –
To bless those, we help -
We bless ourselves.
Finding that –
Angel Inside of us.

Avenues

Alone, I walk in the morning sun.
I find there're many roads to venture to.
Not sure where I'm going,
For there're many directions
To follow through.

With so much before me,
I find things can change
From one minute to the next.
And I'm learning life
Is all about passing the test.

I ask the Lord to be my teacher.
I ask the Lord to be my guide.
And no matter what my life may be -
I feel His Love inside.

Alone, I walk in the morning sun,
I find there're many roads to venture to.
Not sure where I'm going,
For there're many directions
To follow through.
There Are Many-
Avenues.

Together

Through the many years –
There's been many storms that have come our way.
Together, as we embrace our differences -
We can endure all things with – *love*.
For as we stand together –
Always *love* will find a way.

*Sometimes We Meet Those Friends Along The Way –
Not Always By Chance –
But Through A Divine Connection.
For Life Is A Journey – There's A Reason For All Things.*

Encouragement

A Message About Encouragement

Go forward with your passion.
There'll always be distractions
That will steer you off your path.
And there'll be disappointments along the way.
Stay Encouraged!

I Cannot Stay Where I Am

This change I find in me,
Empowers me to never give up,
To endure,
With Faith.
And whatever obstacles along the way,
I can overcome.
Today, I own this for self,
And go forward with a new vision
To know all things I dream for,
Hope for,
I can achieve.
I cannot stay where I am.
And I thank you Lord for this.

Road Blocks

As I keep going each day.
I am finding many road blocks along the way.

Whether I go left or right.
Going forward- traveling day or night.

The road blocks are always there.
Feeling helpless and in despair.

Frustrated!
Not knowing what to do.
I remember that prayer is the answer,
And I come to know the Lord
Will see me through.

And as I journey on- I continue on with the
Many road blocks along the way.
And again, I remember to Pray!

For the Lord is never forsaking.
He gives me strength,
And I stay strong.
And as He sees me through- I continue on.
For there are many-
Road Blocks!

Possibilities

Hold on to your dreams
For the possibility to come true.
Never stop believing-
For a *Blessing* may come to you.
And if you find your dreams you reach for -
Seems impossible to achieve -
Continue to hold on to your dreams-
And Believe.
Hold on to-
Possibilities!

The Leap of Faith

Take the leap of *faith* and believe
Each step you take empowers you
To go the distance.
Find strength through each challenge
You so endure.
And when disappointments come,
Receive them as blessings
To keep going even more.
Never give up,
No matter what comes your way,
No matter how difficult the climb.
Just know as you keep going,
His Mercy,
His Love,
Will never fail you.
Take the Leap of Faith
And – *Believe*.

Words Of Encouragement

I awake this day encouraged.
To know I can do all things possible with You.
For I cannot go back to where I was.
Nor can I stay where I am.
But as I move forward-
I hold on to the promise.

Your Blessings never cease.
And Your Enduring Promise is the reassurance
There's nothing You can't do.

I can rise above any storm imaginable.
I can overcome any obstacle.
My faith is renewed.
And more than ever before I trust in- You!
I Awake Each Day-
Encouraged!

A Journey Of A Thousand Steps

You must never give up when it seems so far.
You must never doubt when it all seems it's going nowhere.
You must never say you can't- always say you can.
It doesn't matter how long the journey.
What matters that you give it your all? -
All the way to the end.
A true winner never gives up,
Never doubts when things go wrong.
Always gearing with positive energy,
No matter how the road turns.
For one single step leads to a thousand steps,
Making dreams come true.

The Beauty Of You

As you come to love who you are-
All you can give-
The beauty of you will shine even more.

Only you can define the gift
That is yours alone.
And when you begin to see the inner you-
Having the Faith in all you can be -
You can rise above any challenge imaginable.

As you come to love who you are-
As you embrace your own uniqueness-
You will always give the best of who you are.
And the beauty of you will always-
Shine Through!

A Message About Faith

Faith is all about believing.
With *faith* - you put your trust in God
To know that He loves you for your own uniqueness-
For you are wonderfully made.
Faith is when you believe without a doubt –
That what is impossible – is possible.
Faith is all about –
Believing!

*Stay Encouraged And Always Keep The Faith.
Take The Disappointments Along the Way —
And Move Forward To Each New Day That
Can Bring Endless Possibilities For You To Discover.*

As We Discover Love

As We Discover Love

Through the storms that we've endured –
Let's press forward to a new beginning.
For more better days are yet to come.

With hope and the faith that what we once had –
The gathering with family and friends
For the holidays.
Spending time seeing a friend just to chat
And to share the breeze of the day.

Seeing each other for birthdays, weddings, graduations,
Or even going to church on Sundays –
As we embrace each other with a smile or a hug.
These things we will have again.

And as we look up to Him - we can smile –
And we can find peace within.

For with the storms behind us –
And what may come tomorrow –
We'll be alright –
As We Discover Love.

Beyond The Sunset

As I look beyond the beautiful skies-
Before the night begins to fall-
I hold on to *hope* for brighter tomorrows.

Where hope lies-
I believe we can hold on to love.
For *hope* invites us to know- *Love!*

Love! is our true salvation.
Love will never fail us-
Only encourages us to see
Its beauty-
To give the best of ourselves-
To always answer to our hearts.

Love will always be there
For each of us to embrace.
And as we come to love
One another –
To believe in its promise-
Love! we can come to know-
Beyond The Sunset.

For The Light Of The World-
A Child Is Born

One Christmas morn-
A child was born.
A sweet child who's light
Will show the way.
Born that day-
A star shined so bright.
Born that day –
That one Christmas morn.
In Bethlehem where all lay still -
Peace and calm-
His Light for all to know so well.

A child was born that day-
That one Christmas morn -
Bringing us peace and love.
Peace and Love to *All the World.*
Jesus!
Precious Child!
The Light Of The World! -
A Child Is Born.

A Message About Christmas

Christmas is about giving and sharing.
Christmas –
A time of family and friends getting together
In the spirit of love for one another.

Whether its decorating the tree –
Baking cookies –
And eating as many as you like -
Or finding that perfect gift -
No matter how large are small -
For it comes with love.

Christmas is also a time of reflection -
As we spend time with those we love -
We create memories we will always hold dear
In our hearts.

Christmas is about giving and sharing.
Christmas also reminds us to always
Carry the love in our hearts.
And when we see with love –
Love we'll always find.
For Love is what Christmas is all about.

Our Saving Grace

May we break bread together you and me.
May we come to a place, as we bring our
Concerns, our fears, our worries to the
Understanding we are in this together.

May we break bread together you and me.
May we bless the time together.
May we listen with open minds and caring hearts.

May we break bread together you and me.
May we tear down the walls of division,
And see more than ever before we need each other.
May we hear both sides to find a way.

May we break bread together you and me.
May we begin here where we are right now,
And carry each other - all the way through.

For as we stand together – all is possible
With faith and The Grace Of God -
Our Saving Grace –
We will survive!
May We Break Bread Together.

Each Day I Awake

The world is most beautiful
When the sun shines on a-
Snow- capped winter's morning.

The world is most beautiful
When spring is in full bloom -
Trees of Cherry Blossoms -
And gardens of flowers all around.

The world is most beautiful
When summer nights showcase the stars above-
No matter where you are.

The world is most beautiful
When autumn leaves keep falling
On those cool days just before winter.

And the world is most beautiful -
Each day I awake -
I still see *Love* no matter
Where I may be-
I see *Love* –
With the hope for an even brighter tomorrow-
Each Day I Awake.

A Message About Love

As you open your heart –
As you see with love –
You'll find fulfillment.
It's about having basic trust –
To first see with an open mind -
An open heart -
That always starts with you.

To be of love -
To let go.
And as you do –
Inner peace you'll always have –
Each time you go with – *Love!*

The Beauty Of Love

As you love, you live fulfilled.
And as you give love, you encourage
Others to give too.
But remember, there're times when love
May not be accepted or received by some.
And sometimes you may feel if it's worth the try.
But just stop and think
As you turn a negative situation
To a positive one,
You'll find much peace, much joy
You can ever imagine when you always
Answer to your heart.
Can you ever imagine anything greater?
For that's-
The Beauty of Love.

Always Love

Sometimes you may not see *Love* present.
And sometimes love seems as though
It doesn't stay around too long.
But when you find there's no Love around-
Hold on to it more than ever.
It's the only thing that- Last.

The world cannot live without Love -
And what's so amazing -
It never lets you down.
The more you invite love -
The more you share love-
Wonderful things happen!

Never give up on *Love*.
Hold on to it more than ever-
For it's the only thing that *–Last!*

Inspiration

To believe all is possible,
That seems impossible,
To always encourage,
To enlighten the spirit,
To spread a little love wherever you go.
And just maybe as you pass it on,
The world will be more beautiful.
And before you know what a difference
You've made.
A more beautiful world you can ever
Have dreamed.
If you could only imagine
Such an inspiration that would be?

Caring

Caring is about giving of your heart.
It's all about compassion, support, and love.
Caring is thinking of others, being a friend
When a friend needs you the most.

Caring is patience, kindness and much more.
And when the world seems unkind,
Always with a loving heart – caring is the sunshine
That comes through.

Caring is about giving of your heart.
And what's most beautiful about caring,
Is that it encourages us to hope for the world
To be a better place –
Each time one cares.

Love Will Always Be There
For Each Of Us To Embrace.
And As We Come To Discover Love –
May We Come To A Place To Love One Another.
LOVE –
Is The Only Thing That Last!

CPSIA information can be obtained
at www.ICGtesting.com
Printed in the USA
BVHW032100280222
630298BV00003B/27

9 781669 807353